# SKYLANDERS UNIVERSE™

# BOOK OF KAOS

GROSSET & DUNLAP
Penguin Young Readers Group
An Imprint of Penguin Random House LLC

Written by Barry Hutchison

Special thanks to Chris Bruno

ISBN 978-0-448-48772-4                                                                                    10 9 8 7 6 5 4 3 2 1

# BOOK OF KAOS

**GROSSET&DUNLAP**
An Imprint of Penguin Random House

# CONTENTS

# WELCOME!

## FROM KAOS

Greetings, fools!

It is I, Lord Kaos, Dark Portal Master and all-around terrifying (yet devastatingly handsome) evil genius. Glumshanks informs me that those ridiculous Skylanders have released a series of books all about themselves and their Elements. Ha! I SAY *HA!*

Anything they can do, I can do a million times better, so I've written a book of my own. So! Utterly destroy those Books of Elements, and prepare yourselves for the most incredible read of your worthless lives!

BEHOLD: *The Book of Kaos.* Yes, my long-awaited, incredible manifesto is packed with never-before-known facts on the creepiest, slimiest, most deliciously disgusting, diabolical creatures to have ever squirmed, wriggled, or stomped across Skylands. You'll also find *TRUE* stories about the fascinating events that made me the ultimate evil overlord that I am today!

NOW, PITIFUL HUMAN FOOLS, steady your nerves, take a deep breath, strap yourselves in, and prepare to be AMAZED. I trust that this glimpse into my fearful presence will leave you so impressed that you will all bow down to ME, the one and only LORD KAOS.

~~Hugs and Kisses,~~
*Doom Always*

Kaos (Lord)

# THE DARKNESS

Imagine this: It's a sunny day. You're out for a walk, minding your own business, when—what's this?—an enormous black cloud passes overhead. You think it's about to rain, because you are an IMBECILE! That's not a rain cloud, it's The Darkness. Don't you know anything?

Nobody knows where The Darkness came from. Not even me! Unbelievable, I know, seeing as I *am* an all-knowing genius. Some believe the Ancients whipped it up by mistake while messing around with Magic. Glumshanks thinks The Darkness came to Skylands on vacation and got lost. That's because, like you, Glumshanks is a FOOL!

Who cares how it got here? The important thing is that it did, and now it floats around causing mischief and mayhem all over the place. What's not to like about that? I feel especially evil when The Darkness tries to destroy the Core of Light, or corrupt those miserable do-gooding Skylanders to the ways of evil! HA-HA-HA!

It's been said that a certain brilliantly diabolical genius (that would be ME) has, in the past, drawn on the power of The Darkness to aid a number of wicked schemes. However, due to the complete and total incompetence of my ridiculous minions, those Sky-LOSERS have somehow managed to stop every one of my ingenious plans. But NO MORE! Soon I will find a way to turn the terrible power of The Darkness against Skylands, and embrace my destiny as Ultimate Evil Overlord of Ultimate DOOM!

# CLOUDCRACKER PRISON

Being a true Dark Portal Master and evil genius, I, KAOS, have no fear whatsoever! That is, with the *slight* possible exception of watching Glumshanks clean his toenails—and, of course, Cloudcracker Prison.

Cloudcracker Prison was once home to some of the most infamously famous evildoers in all of Skylands—the DOOM RAIDERS. With its walls of pure Traptanium—the most impenetrable of all impenetrable substances in Skylands—and guarded by those insufferable Trap Masters, Cloudcracker Prison was built to do only ONE THING: prevent anyone from escaping!

Which is why I blew it up! It was incredible. Ka-BLOOM! The Traptanium may have been tough, but I, KAOS, am even TOUGHER, especially when wielding my Evil Frequency Modulator of Evil DOOM!

Ever since then, the former prisoners of Cloudcracker have been running around causing mayhem. Ah, beautiful mayhem! Unfortunately, some of the inmates developed some serious ego problems while in prison. But fear not, I quickly put them back in their place. HA-HA-HA!

# THE DOOM RAIDERS

Some people would say that the Doom Raiders were the most evil of evildoers to ever spread evil throughout Skylands, but those people would be wrong. Obviously, nobody has ever terrified the easily conquered subjects of Skylands NEARLY as awesomely as I have. However, since I, Lord Kaos, am generous, I suppose I can allow them to have SOME infinitely small recognition for their contribution to evil.

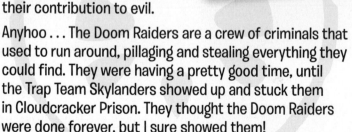

Anyhoo . . . The Doom Raiders are a crew of criminals that used to run around, pillaging and stealing everything they could find. They were having a pretty good time, until the Trap Team Skylanders showed up and stuck them in Cloudcracker Prison. They thought the Doom Raiders were done forever, but I sure showed them!

Now these outlaws are running amok in Skylands again, and for some reason, they don't seem to be eternally grateful to me for setting them free. *Hmph.* At any rate, if you're hoping to be a real evil master of evil someday, I guess I could introduce you to this band of bad guys.

# GULPER

## DOOM FILE

- A blubbery blue sea slug
- Constantly hungry and thirsty
- Proudly wears the Crown of Gluttony
- Really stupid. And I mean really, *really* stupid

## DID YOU KNOW?

Gulper loves soda, and the more of it he drinks, the bigger he grows. His love for the sugary drink also explains why he has only eight teeth.

Although the extra size he gains from the soda's fizzy goodness gives him great strength, the drink is also the source of one of his main weaknesses. Because of the vast amount of soda he guzzles, Gulper must always be aware of where the closest bathroom is located.

# CHOMPY MAGE

## DOOM FILE

- A wizard who hatched from inside a Chompy Pod
- Absolutely, positively, 100 percent obsessed with Chompies
- Has a Chompy glove puppet on one hand at all times
- Dreams of turning everyone in Skylands into Chompies

## DID YOU KNOW?

As well as controlling Chompies, being able to turn into a huge Chompy himself, and having the ability to see through the eyes of any Chompy in Skylands, the Chompy Mage is also the founder of the Chompy Fan Club. And if all of this sounds crazy—IT IS! HA!

Every week, the sad and ridiculous members of the Chompy Fan Club meet in a secret location to discuss all the latest developments in the world of Chompies, swap Chompy stories, and generally just babble nonstop about Chompies. As well as being the founder of the club, the Chompy Mage is currently its one and only member, although he's deluded enough to think he can talk his brother, the Sheep Mage, into joining.

13

# CHEF PEPPER JACK

## DID YOU KNOW?

The fiery Pepper Jack was once the most famous chef in all of Skylands. He'd travel across the land, whipping up delicious treats in front of audiences who flocked by the thousands to see him. He wrote three recipe books—*Things I've Cooked*; *Other Things I've Cooked*; and *Things I Might Cook in the Future*—and all three went on to be best sellers.

Since embracing evil in all its delicious forms, Chef Pepper Jack has left his literary career behind, and instead spends his time blowing things to smithereens. However, he still seems to be grateful to the fans who bought his cookbooks, and if you approach him with one, he'll be happy to sign it. Um, assuming, of course, that he doesn't leave you holding a giant pepper bomb instead.

## DOOM FILE

- For those who like their bad guys extra spicy
- Was once a celebrity chef, but then he developed a taste for evil
- Cooks up all manner of deadly delicacies in his kitchen
- Whisks, chops, blends, and lightly poaches the forces of justice

# DREAMCATCHER

## DOOM FILE

- A floating head from the Realm of Dreams
- Can enter your mind while you sleep, and bring your nightmares to life
- Has a mischievous nature and loves to play sinister pranks
- Has been known to drive whole villages insane for fun

## DID YOU KNOW?

Before being locked up in Cloudcracker Prison, Dreamcatcher had already escaped from one jail—Lucid Lockdown in the Realm of Dreams. While life in Lucid was pretty terrible, it was nothing compared to what awaited her in Cloudcracker.

You see, the other prisoners, being evil villains, actually enjoyed having their nightmares brought to life. The prison was otherwise pretty boring, and her dream-animating ability was top-notch entertainment—they couldn't get enough! But Dreamcatcher soon realized that messing with others' dreams was only fun if it bothered them. Instead, *she* was the one being bothered!

At least, until the night she almost melted their brains into their boots! After that they tended to leave her alone.

**15**

# DR. KRANKCASE

## DOOM FILE

- A Tech creature of unknown origin. With a big hat.
- Although he's a doctor, nobody is exactly sure what kind of doctor he is
- Created a weird green goo that can bring wooden objects to life
- Loves engineering, world domination, and pickles

## DID YOU KNOW?

After Dr. Krankcase lost his legs (he's always misplacing things), he put his incredible engineering skills to use and built himself a new set.

His first attempt backfired badly, after he tried to fit his feet with powerful hidden springs. On his first test walk, both springs accidentally activated, propelling him through the ceiling of his lab.

Not only did the impact give Dr. Krankcase a serious concussion, it also completely ruined his hat. So, to avoid such a thing happening again, the bad doctor went back to the drawing board, and designed the wooden spiderlike legs he scuttles around on today. This boldly evil move not only permanently enshrined him in my awesome *Book of Kaos*, it also meant he'd never wear regular pants again. HA-HA-HA!

# WOLFGANG

## DOOM FILE

- A red-furred werewolf who discovered the musical note for pain
- Before his terrifying transformation into a werewolf, he was a handsome musician
- Large, fierce, and mad-dog crazy!
- His evil tunes have been known to make eardrums—and heads—explode

## DID YOU KNOW?

Although his weapon and musical instrument of choice is the ax-harp he lovingly carved from solid lumps of bone, Wolfgang is equally terrifying at the piano, trombone, and banjo.

In fact, when he's not trying to destroy everything and everyone in Skylands, Wolfgang has been known to go stomping around as a one-man band. He can occasionally be found on busy street corners, booming, clanging, twanging, and causing such a diabolical din that the street empties of pedestrians in seconds—as they flee in terror!

Ever the optimist, Wolfgang always puts an upturned hat on the ground in front of him when he plays, hoping for gold. To date, no money has ever been placed inside it.

# GOLDEN QUEEN

## DOOM FILE

- Leader of the Doom Raiders
- Greedy—she has a desire for all things gold
- Thinks nothing of turning innocent people into precious metal
- Easily angered and does not tolerate failure

## DID YOU KNOW?

The Golden Queen's desire for gold knows no bounds whatsoever. She'll go anywhere, do anything, and hurt anyone if it means getting her hands on even a single coin of the shiny stuff.

Once, a band of pirates caught her fiddling with their treasure chest, which they'd believed was safely buried. The Squidface Brute crew didn't take kindly to thieves (which is ironic, as they'd originally stolen the treasure themselves) and decided to teach her a lesson.

Little did they know, the Golden Queen can absorb gold into her body to make herself bigger, so after absorbing all their precious booty, she kicked them all in their precious booties. Get it? *Booties!* HA-HA-HA!

# LUMINOUS

## DOOM FILE

- Evil Overlord of the Light Element
- He's got star power ... from an actual star!
- Went mad trying to find the ultimate source of light
- Extremely afraid of the dark

## DID YOU KNOW?

The Light Element, along with its Dark counterpart, was hidden in the foundation of Skylands until the destruction of Cloudcracker Prison. The Doom Raider Luminous then reappeared, determined to reclaim his power over the Light Element.

Before he was banished, Luminous spent years fighting darkness and running away from his own shadow. He attempted to steal the Starlight from Radiant City, but wasn't prepared for its guardian, the Trap Master Knight Light. The two battled for days, but eventually, Luminous was defeated and imprisoned within Sunscraper Spire.

Luminous will do whatever it takes to regain control over the Light, even if he has to resort to trickery and deception! I mean, who wouldn't—right?

# NIGHTSHADE

## DOOM FILE

- A thief, and follower of darkness
- Most famous burglar in all of Skylands
- Charming, sneaky, and a bit full of himself
- Steals things for the fun of it

## DID YOU KNOW?

Like Luminous, Nightshade's Element was hidden from Skylands for ages before reappearing. Unlike Luminous, Nightshade doesn't take himself quite so seriously. He loves doing evil, but not because he needs to—just because he can.

Nightshade might seem *too* charming and charismatic to be a Doom Raider (though of course not NEARLY as charming as I, LORD KAOS), but don't be deceived. Although he appears to be a gentleman, he enjoys showing off his ninja skills in battle, and feels no remorse for his victims.

To Nightshade, life is just a game—a game that he intends to win!

# LIGHT

If there's one thing I really hate, it's the Core of Light and those annoying Skylanders. Yes, yes, that's two things, but I hate them both the same, so they share first place.

The Core of Light was built by the Ancients long ago, and has only one function—to fill the skies with horribly pure light and keep The Glorious Darkness at bay. I mean . . . seriously? Where's the fun in that?

The Core is made up of the eight Eternal Sources—mystical objects, each one aligned to a different Element—and has stood for thousands of years, vomiting its disgusting light up into the air and keeping Skylands safe from evil. At least, until I smashed it to bits with the help of my big four-headed dragon. HA-HA-HA-HA!

I mean, yes, the Skylanders managed to put it all back together again before I could complete my glorious plan and achieve the victory that I—Kaos—so richly deserve. Normally, I'd just blame Glumshanks, but I know this time it was that fool Eon. But one day, he will pay. He and all of those miserable Sky-LAME-OS!

**Magic**   **Fire**   **Life**   **Air**   **Earth**   **Undead**   **Tech**   **Water**

# THE ARKEYANS

I'll get into much more detail about the Arkeyans later, when I grace you with my vast, encyclopedic knowledge of evil beings in Skylands.

For now, all you need to know is that the Arkeyans lived long, long ago, and were masters of the Magic and Tech Elements. They used their knowledge to create some pretty powerful machinery. If only they had been as brilliant as I am, they might have learned how to make super-weapons using *all* of the Elements! Still, they did their best.

So let's take a look at two particularly nasty pieces of Arkeyan Tech, because, as you know, *nasty* is right up my alley.

## Arkeyan Conquertron

Ah, the Conquertron—one of my greatest allies in my never-ending war on Skylands. Until he exploded, anyway. He wasn't much use after that.

The Conquertron was constructed thousands of years ago by the Arkeyans, in order to ensure the enslaved Mabu didn't mess around when they should be working. Considering the Mabu are tiny, building the biggest robot in history to watch over them was probably overkill, but who am I to judge? What am I saying? I'm KAOS! I'm the PERFECT judge. HA-HA-HA!

Although immensely powerful, the Conquertron was defeated by the Skylander Giants and left to rust. There he would have stayed, had my genius not restored him to his full glory.

With his help, I came *so* close to seizing control of Skylands! And then it all went wrong, and my faithful Conquertron shut down and crashed into an isolated island. Sigh. It's so hard for an ultimate evil overlord to find good help these days.

# The Iron Fist of Arkus

The Iron Fist of Arkus was worn by the ancient Arkeyan Kings, and was an incredible fusion of Magic and Tech that granted the wearer unimaginable power.

The legend goes that when the Arkeyans first took over Skylands, they overheard someone saying they "ruled with an iron fist." Worried that they didn't actually have an iron fist, and not wanting to embarrass themselves, they quickly built one.

Donning the Iron Fist of Arkus gives the wearer complete control over the Arkeyan Army. I found this out for myself when I put it on and was instantly transformed into a huge, hulking—and devastatingly attractive—giant robot!

Despite my defeat (which in no possible way was my own fault), the Iron Fist of Arkus remains one of the most devastating weapons in all of Skylands. If only I could find out where those sneaky Skylanders have hidden it . . .

# THE WONDERS OF PETRIFIED DARKNESS

Imagine if you can, young Portal Master Impostor, a form of evil so intense that it became an actual solid thing. Your limited imagination probably can't picture such a thing, but luckily, it doesn't have to. Solidified evil already exists. Behold the wonder of Petrified Darkness!

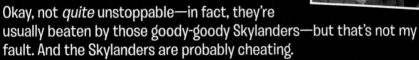

Recently, a certain diabolical genius (me) discovered a way of using the Petrified Darkness to turn otherwise harmless goody-two-shoes types into unstoppable agents of evil!

Okay, not *quite* unstoppable—in fact, they're usually beaten by those goody-goody Skylanders—but that's not my fault. And the Skylanders are probably cheating.

Anyway, my point is: If you absolutely have to evilize everybody in the room, Petrified Darkness is precisely what you need. Just wear gloves. Trust me.

## EVILIZED ENEMIES

Behold some of the mind-numbingly evil creatures I have created! You will then marvel at my awesome genius in action! Oh yes, you will . . .

### Evilized Boghogs

Boghogs: Even the name is dull. These docile creatures spend all their time snuffling around in their own filth, like Glumshanks on his day off (just kidding—he doesn't get days off).

After I evilized them, however, they became wild, savage beasts! Sadly, the idiotic creatures proved to be of little use to me, especially when they kept running headfirst into walls and knocking themselves out.

# Evilized Sugarbats

Sugarbats are so sickly sweet, they make me sick! Literally. I can barely even eat a whole one these days. With their wide eyes, fluffy fur, and adorable ears, they're loved by almost everyone. Surely no one would be so cruel as to evilize such innocent creatures, right?

Wrong! Once affected by my Petrified Darkness crystals, the Sugarbats went from horribly cute to just plain horrible. Personally, I thought it was an improvement, but those infuriating Skylanders didn't agree, and changed them all back.

# Evilized Screechers

Just like the Sugarbats, only an absolute monster would want to corrupt the harmless tree-dwelling Screechers and turn these noble birds into fearsome flying things of ultimate evil. Fortunately, I *am* an absolute monster, and did just that.

Once twisted to the Dark side, the Screechers let out deafening shrieks and swooped over my enemies, spraying fire. And not just ordinary fire, mind you—*evilized* fire, which is a totally different color and, I don't know, probably hotter or something.

# Evilized Greebles

I finally started to wonder what would happen if I blasted something that was already pretty nasty with Petrified Darkness. Greebles are a pretty mean bunch, but when I zapped them, they turned into the absolute worst of the worst. It was amazing!

While trying to discover the Skylanders' weaknesses, I stumbled upon one of their training manuals. Of course, I stole it, and was surprised to discover there was just one measly page dedicated to me. No matter. Let's see what it has to say about yours truly.

# EXTRACT FROM SKYLANDERS TRAINING MANUAL

## CHARACTER PROFILE: KAOS

**Name:** Kaos

**Age:** Unknown

**Occupation:** Evil ~~genius~~ & Portal Master *So true!*

**Personality:** ~~Arrogant~~, ~~cowardly~~, and often ~~idiotic~~ *These are clearly typos.*

**Strengths:** Dark Magic, control over evil creatures, knowledge of ancient technologies *and good at dancing*

**Weaknesses:** Overconfidence, stupidity, inability to see the glaring flaws in his plans, lack of height *Bit harsh.*

Although little is known of Kaos's early life, rumor has it that he is the descendant of a long line of Dark Portal Masters. While his brothers were gifted with flawless skin and flowing blond locks, Kaos was ~~bald and ugly~~ *differently handsome*, and was shunned by his father, who was disappointed in Kaos's lack of evil instinct, and also appeared to be a hideously misshapen runt. *This is just offensive.*

Abandoning his cruel relatives, Kaos left his family home, accompanied only by his ~~butler~~ *worthless troll*, Glumshanks. While wandering the wilderness, he discovered his ~~reasonably~~ *very* impressive magical abilities, and with Glumshanks ~~assisting~~ *getting in the way all the time* he began to study Dark Magic.

Kaos will stop at nothing in his quest to rule Skylands. While he may come across as clueless, idiotic, and hopelessly inept, he is a real threat to the continued safety of all who inhabit Skylands, and should be taken very seriously, indeed. *Take it easy!*

Most of the time. *What's that supposed to mean?*

# EVIL GENIUS GUIDE

**S**o you think you've got what it takes to be an evil genius? Ha! You don't know the first thing about the role of a diabolical mastermind.

Luckily for you, benevolent evil Lord KAOS is on hand to lead you down the path of Darkness. Throughout this book, I'll be on hand to give you advice about how to turn yourself from an insignificant nobody into a true evil genius, feared the world over. Let's start with the basics . . .

## Looking the Part

Take a look at the picture of me. Doesn't everything about me just scream *evil*? From the black robe to the terrifyingly sharp teeth, everything about my look is carefully planned to convey a sense of awesome wickedness.

Now, imagine if instead of that black robe, I'd opted for a pink dress with yellow flowers on it. It wouldn't have been as effective, would it? That's just one of the common mistakes that evil geniuses in training can make, but you can avoid them by following my guide.

## Appropriate Things for an Evil Genius to Wear

- A black robe
- A *very* dark gray robe
- Face paint
- A lab coat, ideally in black
- Robotic battle armor
- A scary mask
- A jet pack
- An invisibility cape
- Glasses (They make you look more intelligent.)

## Inappropriate Things for an Evil Genius to Wear

- Stilts
- A clown costume
- A beard of bees
- Anything with a target embroidered over the heart
- A pair of ballet shoes four sizes too small
- Robotic battle armor set to self-destruct in five seconds
- A heart-shaped brooch with I LOVE BUNNIES written on it
- An enormous diaper
- Novelty slippers
- Electric-shock pants

Armed with that advice, you should have no excuse not to at least *look* like an evil genius. Keep reading to continue your training, my young apprentice!

We've already seen what the Skylanders training manual had to say about yours truly, and even though most of it was completely wrong, let's see what it has to say about my troll butler, Glumshanks.

# CHARACTER PROFILE: GLUMSHANKS

**Name:** Glumshanks

**Age:** Unknown

**Species:** Troll

**Occupation:** Butler to Lord Kaos

**Personality:** Loyal, cautious, and sensible
*and utterly infuriating*

**Strengths:** Reasonably strong, level-headed, ~~more~~ intelligent than his master, Kaos
*much less*

**Weaknesses:** Cowardly, downtrodden, obeys without question
*personal hygiene*

Although trolls are usually obsessed with blowing things to pieces, Glumshanks could never quite work out which end of the dynamite to light. As a result, he (flunked all his classes at the Troll academy,) and was forced to leave the school in shame.
*He never told me this!*          **HA-HA-HA!**

After his first educational failure, he was sent to study at a school of magical villainy, where he was the first troll

ever to attend. There he met a young Kaos, who ~~pitifully begged~~ *I wouldn't go that far*
Glumshanks to be his evil servant. Kaos promised the troll that
he would help him establish his own evil domain, but he has not
followed through on this offer. *Why would I? Glumshanks is utterly useless.*

Since then, Glumshanks has continued to serve Kaos **very badly**
and is usually tied up in his plans one way
or another. It

appears that
Glumshanks may also
~~be the closest thing
Kaos has to a friend.~~

*Not true! I've got loads.*
While Glumshanks
may not be
particularly
dangerous, he was *by his genius master*
once evilized and came very close to defeating the Skylanders in
battle. After that, though, the troll seemed content to go back
to washing Kaos's socks and obeying the evil Portal Master's
~~ridiculous whims.~~ *badly*

## How dare they??

# AN OPEN EVIL LOVE LETTER TO ROLLER BRAWL

I don't consider all of the Skylanders to be my enemies. One of them—Roller Brawl—I like to think of as my future wife. For some reason she doesn't see things the same way, and is able to resist my charms despite the letter I sent her to demonstrate my gentle, caring side. I have no idea why the letter didn't work—take a look for yourself and see my mastery of the written word in action.

ATTENTION, ROLLER BRAWL!

It is I, Lord Kaos, master of evil and future ruler of all Skylands. You may remember me from that time I said hello to you at the Undead Roller Derby League, or from that other occasion when I had your idiotic brothers kidnapped by Drow.

They're fine, by the way. Probably. I haven't checked on them in a while, but I'm sure they're doing as well as can be expected. Hanging upside down by your toes this long would spoil anyone's mood, am I right?!

But I digress . . .

I am writing this letter to give you an opportunity to turn your back on those stupid Skylanders and join me in my never-ending quest to do terrible things and rule Skylands as its ultimate evil overlord! As you know, I'm ruggedly handsome and a stylish dresser, but here are some things about me you may not know.

**I have a great sense of humor!** When Glumshanks fell down the stairs last week and hit his head on every single step, I laughed nonstop for over an hour. I was crying at one point, it was so hilarious.

**I like the great outdoors!** When not plotting to destroy the Core of Light and unleash The Glorious Darkness upon Skylands, I enjoy long walks in the wilderness. Well, technically I send Glumshanks because I don't like getting my feet wet, but he enjoys them on my behalf.

**I love animals!** Seriously, I'll eat any of them. Sometimes whole.

I'm not saying we should get married (but we definitely should), I'm just saying we should go on a date sometime. We could look at pictures of me doing impressive things. It would be excellent.

I have attached this letter to a Geargolem who is under instructions to bring you to me alive and, if possible, unharmed. Please do not attempt to resist as it'll really hurt my feelings and I'm surprisingly sensitive for a supreme Dark Overlord of Ultimate Evil.

Hugs and kisses,

Kaos (Lord and soon-to-be-Emperor)

# EVIL GENIUS GUIDE

By now you will probably be wearing a black robe, or at least have drawn all over your face with pen. You're probably saying to yourself, "I feel like a real evil genius!" To which I would reply, "SILENCE!"

Being a diabolical criminal mastermind is about more than having the right wardrobe. Before you can fully embrace the ways of evil, you must first learn to talk like a supervillain.

## Talking the Talk

On the next page, you will find examples of some things you may want to say when you adopt your dastardly new role, and some things you definitely do *not* want to be overheard uttering.

As a general rule, everything you say as an evil genius should be shouted angrily at the top of your lungs. Also, feel free to accompany anything you say with maniacal laughter—it really helps to add emphasis.

## Appropriate Things for an Evil Genius to Say

- Silence!
- Fools!
- Unleash the Trollverines!
- Prepare to be annihilated!
- Activate the destructo-bot!
- Behold my awesome power!
- Bring me everything on the menu, and be quick about it!
- Eat laser!
- You're doomed. DOOMED!

## Inappropriate Things for an Evil Genius to Say

- Run away!
- Don'tcha just love rainbows?
- Yes, I'd very much like to donate to your charity.
- Not the face! Not the face!
- Anyone up for a sing-along?
- Thumbs down for evil!
- I thought I'd leave the last pudding for you.
- Peace out.

So there you have it. You're almost an evil genius. Continue reading to find the final installment later in this book. **OR I WILL DESTROY YOU!**

# TALES OF NEAR VICTORY!

People assume that my encounters with the Skylanders always end in defeat. I say it all depends on how you define "defeat." However, sometimes my plans *do* work, and I come surprisingly close to victory! And when I don't, it's certainly because of some incompetent minions. Like Glumshanks . . .

For example, the time I cunningly teamed up a pack of Bone Chompies with a troop of Bone 'n' Arrows and sent them to take out the Skylanders one at a time. On the face of it, the plan was a work of genius.

Each set of minions brought very different skills to the table—the Bone Chompies could attack close up, while the Bone 'n' Arrows hung back and attacked from a distance. Also, they were all basically skeletons, so they were difficult to hurt and looked really scary all marching together.

To make them even more terrifying, I waited until nightfall before sending them to attack. The Chompies launched an assault on a village while the Bone 'n' Arrows watched for an approaching Skylander. Sure enough, just a few minutes later, one of those goody-goodies came rushing along to help save the village, and the Bone 'n' Arrows got him in their sights.

It should have worked. My loyal minions should have defeated that one Skylander, then gone on to defeat the rest. I should have been ruling Skylands before the night was over, had it not been for just one stroke of bad luck.

The Skylander who came to save the village was Hot Dog, and it turns out that Hot Dog *really* likes to get his teeth into bones. Seriously! Who knew?

Obviously I didn't personally oversee the attack, because I like my beauty sleep, but when I went along to the village in the morning expecting to see my skeletal minions all celebrating, I instead found a few dozen little mounds of earth with the occasional bone poking up through the soil.

Yes, not only had Hot Dog defeated them, he'd then buried them all afterward! How embarrassing for the foolish bony beasts. Fortunately, nobody knew I'd sent them, so I just pretended I had never known a thing about it. Er, until now, I guess. Anyway—bow to my clearly superior evil genius!

So this Skylanders training manual I found seems to be completely useless and filled with inaccuracies. I suppose we may as well take one last look and find out what it has to say about my mother . . .

# CHARACTER PROFILE: KAOS'S MOM

**Name:** Er . . . Kaos's Mom

**Age:** Never ask a lady her age.

**Occupation:** Dark Portal Master

**Personality:** Manipulative, overbearing, arrogant *and embarrassing*

**Strengths:** Intelligence, cunning, ruthlessness

**Weaknesses:** Pride and arrogance *and her overwhelming love for her son. That was sarcasm, by the way.*

Kaos's mother may well be the ~~most~~ *second* evil being who has ever lived. A brilliant *-ish* strategist with a strong grasp of Dark Magic, she has nevertheless been unable to fulfill her dream of conquering Skylands—a fact that greatly frustrates her. *And makes her son laugh.*

It is said that Kaos's mother is deeply unhappy in general. Not only has she failed to achieve her life's goal, but she considers her son to be an ~~immense disappointment~~ *all-around great guy*. Rumor has it that when Kaos was a baby, his mother tried repeatedly to lose him or banish him to faraway lands. Despite this, he somehow always (found his way back home.) *Because I am a genius.* As she is related to Kaos, you might assume that his

mom would share his complete
~~awesomeness~~
and utter ~~incompetence,~~ *awesomeness*
but unlike her son, Kaos's
mother poses a real,
considerable threat
to the safety of all of
Skylands. *So do I!!*

Although she clearly
despises Kaos, *she didn't say*
*that, did she??*
Kaos's mother has a
good relationship with
Glumshanks, and the two enjoy
catching up over tea
and cakes whenever
she comes to visit.

*HA! Try doing that now in*
*a Mirror Prison of Oblivion,*
*Mother!*

# EVIL GENIUS GUIDE

Well now, you've chosen your outfit and you've memorized a few evil-genius phrases. BIG WHOOP! Any fool could do that stuff, even Glumshanks, and he's a complete imbecile.

Just as looking like a Chompy and talking like a Chompy doesn't make you a Chompy (no matter what the Chompy Mage might insist), so too looking and talking like an evil genius doesn't turn you into one. To fully realize your evil-genius potential, you must learn to act correctly. Luckily for you, the greatest evil genius who ever lived is on hand to help you do just that.

## Acting the Part

Acting like an evil genius is not as easy as you might think. It's not all blowing things up and unleashing diabolical plans on an unsuspecting world. Yes, it's *mostly* that, granted, but it's not *all* that.

As well as understanding the types of things you should do, it's important to learn the sorts of things you should never do. There are ways in which a true master of evil would never dream of acting, and if you want to be taken seriously, you should avoid them, too.

## Appropriate Things for an Evil Genius to Do

- Concoct elaborate evil schemes.
- Get a henchman to do the dirty work.
- Build an underground evil lair.
- Turn things into much more unpleasant things.
- Mock the Skylanders.
- Point dramatically.
- Laugh maniacally.
- Make everyday objects huge. And evil.
- Unleash DOOOOOM!

## Inappropriate Things for an Evil Genius to Do

- Help old ladies across the road.
- Carve unicorns out of soap.
- Pick up litter.
- Assist the forces of good.
- Wash their hands after going to the bathroom.
- Write songs about daisies.
- Turn their evil lair into a day care center.
- Dance like no one is watching.

Congratulations, you are now an evil genius! But always remember that I'm a better one.

# KAOS'S JOKES

The first thing people usually comment on when they see me is how good I look. The second thing is usually my commanding presence, or how amazingly evil I am. What people often overlook, though, is my *wickedly hilarious* sense of humor. I'm always cracking incredibly funny jokes, just like these zingers below.

**Q:** Why did Glumshanks cross the road?
**A:** BECAUSE I COMMANDED IT!

**Q:** What do you get if you cross a Drow and a Geargolem?
**A:** I have no idea, but it would make for an interesting experiment and may be of value in my war against the Skylanders. Good suggestion. Well done.

**Q:** How many Trolls does it take to clean a castle?
**A:** One, if you shout at him loudly enough.

**Knock, knock!**
Who's there?
**Lord Kaos, ultimate evil overlord and supreme emperor of Skylands, greatest Dark Portal Master to have ever lived!**
Lord Kaos, ultimate evil overlord and supreme emperor of Skylands, greatest Dark Portal Master to have ever lived who?
**What?**
Sorry?
**Come on, Mother, just open the door.**
You've got the wrong house—go away. Leave us alone.
**Actually, now that I think about it, that last one wasn't actually a joke so much as a painful memory I've spent years trying to forget, but the other three were pure comedy, I'm sure you'll agree. (Otherwise I'll have you destroyed!)**

# GLUMSHANKS'S TO-DO LIST

√ Make breakfast for Lord Kaos.

√ Have breakfast thrown at me.

√ Clean up breakfast.

√ Make the bed.

√ Do the laundry.

√ Duck magical lightning bolt.

√ Iron robes.

√ Prepare lunch.

Point out the flaws in Lord Kaos's latest scheme.

Be completely ignored.

Watch Lord Kaos's latest scheme go horribly wrong.

Resist urge to say "I told you so."

Be struck by magical lightning bolt for no reason.

Prepare dinner.

Put giant ice pack on my head. Again.

# TALES OF NEAR VICTORY!

Fine, okay, I'll admit that in that last tale I told you about the Bone Chompies and the Bone 'n' Arrows, it's somewhat possible that my ingenious plan didn't completely work out as intended, but there were other occasions when I definitely did almost emerge victorious from an encounter with the Skylanders.

Take, for example, the time I used Petrified Darkness to evilize that ridiculous, meat-headed imbecile Flynn. Ha, you didn't know about *that*, did you?

For some reason, as well as turning Flynn evil, the Petrified Darkness did something unexpected—it made him intelligent. Obviously not as intelligent as I am—because NO ONE is as intelligent as I am—but a definite improvement on his usual enchilada-gorging buffoonery.

With his enhanced brainpower and his newly developed appreciation for evil, Flynn slipped into camp and sneakily stole away the weapons of every Skylander in sight.

Flynn then told the Skylanders he was going to demonstrate a magic trick he had learned—one which involved each and every one of them being tied up! For a moment, it looked as if they suspected something was wrong—Flynn was glowing purple with evilized energy, after all—but they assumed Flynn was clowning around as usual, and this was just part of the show.

When he had the Skylanders tied up, Flynn told them he had to step outside to complete the trick. Once outside, the plan was for Flynn to signal to me by firing a rocket from Zook's stolen bazooka into the air, at which point I would come swooping in with an army of Trolls.

Unfortunately, Flynn's clumsiness reared its ugly head at that very moment, and he held the bazooka upside down. Instead of the rocket shooting up into the air, it shot backward and exploded at his feet.

The force of the blast set his pants on fire, knocked him out, and rid him of all that lovely evilized energy. By the time I decided to go charging in with the Trolls to find out what the holdup was, he had managed to untie the Skylanders.

The Trolls took the thrashing of their lives, but I managed to avoid a beating, because as well as being an evil genius and the greatest Portal Master to have ever lived, I am also highly skilled at effective escape maneuvers.

# KAOS'S MOM'S DIARY

**P**ssst! Glumshanks here. Look, I'm sneaking in these pages because I think it's time people know exactly why Lord Kaos acts the way he does. Oh sure, on the surface he may seem just like an ordinary, everyday megalomaniacal evil overlord who wants to conquer Skylands and rule it with an iron fist (and that's his good side)—but having been his butler for a long time, I'm here to tell you that there's much more to him than that. To really get a sense of what's going on inside Lord Kaos, take a look at this excerpt from his mother's diary. Don't get me wrong, I like Kaos's mother a lot (in fact, there's no one I'd rather have tea with), but she's never exactly been the picture of a "loving mother"—if you get my meaning. Just see for yourself.

### Diary Entry #1

How disappointing. You would think that being born to the most diabolical family of Dark Portal Masters that ever lived would eventually rub off on a child—but apparently you'd be mistaken. Generations of evil blood running through his veins, yet he can't grasp even the basics of villainy? I'd better put him in the dungeon for a few days. Maybe he'll have something to show for it when he gets out.

### Diary Entry #2

Apparently, rather than spending his confinement learning something actually evil, he decided to play with wooden puppets. PLAY? Most pathetic of all, he isn't even able to make them actually do his bidding. Any decent Dark Portal Master would have them under control by now, but he seems destined to be utterly incompetent forever. At any rate, I'm going to take advantage of his distraction and go out for a little ME time.

## Diary Entry #3

Whoops! I may have gotten a little carried away with my ME time. After a couple of days destroying islands and utterly terrorizing the area, I figured it was time to return to check on the child. It turns out he may have some puny "magical" abilities after all. He managed to bring his little wooden puppets to life, and when I returned, they were dancing all around the castle. What an annoying scene it was. I can't wait until he is old enough to send away to Dark Portal Master School.

## Diary Entry #4

The fool somehow created a giant holographic projection of his head, and insisted on projecting it at the dinner table. He clearly believes it is quite a good trick, though it is actually just a trifling nuisance that a baby could do. I was capable of much more sinister feats at his age. At any rate, it was quite irritating, so it's off to the dungeon again!

## Diary Entry #5

I can't take it anymore. I'm sending him to Dark Portal Master School. Technically, he won't be old enough to attend for several more years, but I can't risk anyone in the family seeing what has happened to our grand legacy of supremely diabolical evil. I've been assured by the Headmaster that he can whip Kaos into shape. I'm also thinking about sending Glumshanks with him. I mean, a boy needs his butler after all. Besides, I need SOMEONE I can trust to keep an eye on him.

# MORE VILE VILLAINS

While I'm by far the greatest villain in all of Skylands, I'm by no means the only one.

I came across a slew of recently escaped villains, who seem tougher—yet stupider—than the usual fiendish nasties. Rumor says these idiotic wannabes let themselves be trapped by the Skylanders. And some people even say that they've been brainwashed into doing *good deeds*.

Obviously, these baddies are nowhere near as clever or interesting as I am, but in the unlikely event you want to know more, here's what I've been able to find out.

## Fire Villains

### Grinnade

I do so love seeing someone happy at their work, and Grinnade always looks delighted to be blowing things up—particularly if those *things* are the Skylanders.

### Scrap Shooter

An Evilikin with out-of-the-ordinary hands, Scrap Shooter uses his arm-cannons to blast high-speed chunks of metal junk and garbage at his enemies.

## Smoke Scream

Ahhh, those Trolls and their wonderful machines! Strutting around in this powerful mech-suit, Smoke Scream can zap enemies with his plasma beam or blow them up with missiles.

# Life Villains

### Broccoli Guy

Much like the food he resembles, Broccoli Guy is a healthy choice—if he's on your side. When he's not trying to hurt his enemies, he's busy healing his friends with the mighty power of vegetables.

### Chompy

When it comes to villains, they don't get more classic than the Chompies. These bitey-faced fiends have been doing my bidding since day one, and this guy is meaner than most.

### Cuckoo Clocker

This big-beaked bird is all about the clobbering. With his suit of armor, huge hands, and earsplitting screech, he's a real feathered fiend.

### Sheep Creep

He may look like just an ordinary sheep, because he is actually just an ordinary sheep. He does have guns, though, so that's something, at least.

### Shield Shredder

You might think you're safe from Shield Shredder, but here's some advice—you're never safe from Shield Shredder. His buzz-saw attack can rip right through the strongest defenses.

# Tech Villains

## Brawlrus

A muscle-packed pirate with a 'stache to die for, Brawlrus is a walrus who'd really like to maul us. Well, maul you, anyway. I'm sure he has no problem with me.

## Bruiser Cruiser

Trolls are pretty dangerous at the best of times, but shove one behind the controls of a giant boxing robot and prepare to be introduced to a whole new world of pain.

## Mab Lobs

You probably think all Mabu are cute and cuddly, don't you? Because you are a FOOL! Mab Lobs comes from a delightfully twisted alternate dimension and enjoys nothing more than blowing up goody-goodies.

## Shrednaught

Take two Trolls, place them inside a heavily armored machine with an enormous chainsaw mounted on the front, and what have you got? No legs, probably.

## Trolling Thunder

Trolling Thunder trundles around in an armored tank, shooting enemies who are far away, and running over any that get too close.

# Water Villains

## Brawl & Chain

Another walrus who has embraced the
ways of evil, this big-tusked brute
has hooks, balls, and chains
instead of hands, and uses them to do all manner of nasty stuff.

## Chill Bill

Chill Bill is a crazy Troll with a jet pack and a
supercold ice gun. He also happens to be the
coolest radio DJ in Skylands. (Get it? Cool!)

## Cross Crow

If you cross Cross Crow, chances are you're
going to find yourself on the receiving end of
a blast from his crossbow, or being pecked
to pieces by his flock of bird minions. So
try not to.

## Slobber Trap

He's big! He's bulky! He's a weird sort of dog-
thing made out of rocks! Slobber Trap gets his
name from the disgustingly sticky drool he
dribbles all over the place.

## Threatpack

Once upon a time, Threatpack was a scientific
genius. Nowadays, he's a scientific genius with
an awesome jet pack that shoots rockets,
which is a huge improvement in every way.

# Earth Villains

## Chomp Chest

Hey, a treasure chest—that's great, right? WRONG!
This wooden monstrosity will literally flip its lid as it
attempts to gobble you up whole.

### Grave Clobber

An ancient mummy made out of living stone, Grave
Clobber can smash you with his fists or assault
you with his telekinetic powers. If you're
lucky, he might bandage you up afterward.

## Tussle Sprout

Yuck—sprouts! They're horrible, correct? Well, imagine
a living sprout with an overwhelming desire to do evil!
Suddenly the edible version doesn't seem so bad . . .

# Air Villains

### Bad Juju

This ghostly skeleton can summon storms. She also
likes to sleep, so wake her up and you'll have to
weather the consequences. Ha! See what I did there?

## Buzzer Beak

Aww, look at the cuddly bird in the adorable hat!
Now watch while he pecks your face off! Although
he's quite small, so he'll probably peck your knees off first.

### Krankenstein

Kranky by name and, er, cranky by nature, this
creation of Dr. Krankcase can suck up enemies
with his hands, before the blades in his arm
slice them up sideways. Nice!

# Magic Villains ✦

## Bomb Shell

This turtle-thing is protected by a hard shell that is covered in lots and lots of lovely bombs. His name is actually a complete coincidence, though. What are the chances?

## Pain-Yatta

This magic-powered piñata may have an interior filled with delicious candy, but you'd have to get through his rough 'n' tough exterior first. Good luck with that.

## Rage Mage

Rage Mage is a . . . well, I mean, he's . . . okay, I don't know what he is, exactly. He's evil, he wields magic, and he'll bash you with his staff if you get too close. That's all you need to know.

# Undead Villains 💀

### Bone Chompy

Out of all the Chompies in Skylands, this one is badder than all the rest, and likes to leave traps around to bite people on the feet.

## Hood Sickle

A huge, terrifying reaper who wields a razor-sharp scythe and can teleport in the blink of an eye. He could be standing behind you right now. NO, DON'T LOOK!

### Masker Mind

This floating purple phantom gives Glumshanks the creeps. I, however, am made of sterner stuff, and this psychic spirit doesn't spook me in the slightest.

# Dark Villains

## Eye Scream

A long-haired mutant cyclops with a terrible habit of staring, Eye Scream is 10 percent body, 90 percent eyeball, and 100 percent pure evil.

### Fisticuffs

An Evilikin with a love of punching heroes very hard in the face, which he is very good at thanks to his enormous—and enormously powerful—right hand.

## Tae Kwon Crow

He's a ninja! He leads a band of Sky Pirates! He refers to himself as "The Great Hawkmongous" for reasons not entirely clear! You'd best keep well out of this bird's flight path.

# Light Villains

### Blaster-Tron

Is it a robot from the future? Is it a mysterious alien from another world? Don't ask me. All I know is that Blaster-Tron is a metal marvel, and a real force to be reckoned with.

## Eye Five

Another eye-based mutant. Eye Five doesn't have one eye in the middle of his head, though—he has two eyes in the palms of his hands. It must make clapping absolute agony.

### Lob Goblin

Charged with electrical energy, mess with this explosive-tossing Goblin and you're in for a real shock.

# THE ULTIMATE GUIDE TO VILLAINY

Although I'm sure you would never tire of hearing tales of my fantastic adventures, I *did* promise to devote some of this book to my minions. On the whole, they are incredibly stupid (compared to me), but I fully intend to seize ultimate control of Skylands using some of these utterly brutIsh—and even more disposable—evil creatures.

# GUIDE TO SPELL PUNKS

Spell Punks are powerful wizards who use magic to cause trouble for do-gooders everywhere. While they originally shied away from directly engaging in battle, recently they've started to toughen up a little and face the Skylanders head-on.

### Air Spell Punks

Summoning tornadoes that can harm heroes and protect villains is mere child's play to an Air Spell Punk.

### DOOM FACT

You don't want to know what Spell Punks look like with their hoods off. Ugh!

### Water Spell Punks

Their magical control over the Water Element allows these little wizard-types to freeze Skylosers in their tracks.

### Earth Spell Punks

With their magical powers over the Earth Element, these wizards can create rocky shields to protect their allies.

### Life Spell Punks

Even the toughest villains usually end up taking a beating from the Skylanders. Luckily, the Life Spell Punks are on hand to heal their wounds.

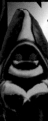

### Tech Spell Punks

Armed with unique Tech-based powers, these Spell Punks can conjure up a hovering laser device to blast Skylanders.

### Undead Spell Punks

When not shooting skulls at their enemies, Undead Spell Punks can summon skeletal Trolls and other baddies, and send them to do their bidding.

### Fire Spell Punks

For being infused with the blazing hot power of Fire, Fire Spell Punks don't really take full advantage of it. Instead they use their power to light dynamite. They really must try harder.

### Magic Spell Punks

A Magic Spell Punk can turn minions invisible, letting them get the drop on any unsuspecting Skylander.

### Time Spell Punks

This variety has complete mastery of time itself, and can stop and start it as they see fit. They can also shoot fireballs, which is handy.

### DID YOU KNOW?

Time Spell Punks are not aligned with an Element, which keeps Skylosers on their toes.

# GUIDE TO CYCLOPSES

Cyclopses come in all shapes and sizes, but are easy to identify due to A) their one eye, and B) their terrible smell. Most of them are utterly evil, but a handful have elected to side with the Skylanders. The traitors!

### Timidclopses

These little ones would rather jump off a cliff than face an enemy in direct battle. Much like my cowardly servant Glumshanks.

### DID YOU KNOW?

The idiot Cyclopses once tried to build a ship from stone!

### Cyclops Choppers

Wielding axes, these Cyclopses attack by spinning around, chopping up anything that gets too close . . . before eventually getting dizzy and falling over.

### Bag O' Booms

These one-eyed wonders carry bombs that they will happily hurl at anyone they don't like the look of.

### Armored Mohawks

This type is much like the Cyclops Choppers, only with a shock of sticking-up hair.

### Coldspear Cyclopses

Rather than risk getting dizzy and falling over, these Cyclopses jab at enemies with their spears.

### Cyclops Gazermages

These wizard-like one-eyes are able to focus the heat from the sun into concentrated beams.

### Twistpick Cyclopses

What is it with Cyclopses and spinning? This variety twirls around while carrying a heavy pickax.

### Cyclops Dragons

Part skeleton, part Cyclops, part dragon, all very dangerous.

### Cyclops Spinners

These spinning Cyclopses carry pointy, scary-looking knives instead of axes.

### Cyclops Snowblasters

These spiky little turrets do exactly what their name suggests. It's like having a snowball fight with a machine, but more dangerous!

### Cyclops Sleetthrowers

If these Cyclopses were good guys, they'd use their shovels to clear little old ladies' sidewalks.

Instead, they shovel up snow and throw it at Skylanders!

### Cyclops Brawlbucklers

Equipped with a shield and a heavy studded mace, it's hard to believe that these Cyclopses could ever be taken down by a Skylander.

# GUIDE TO TROLLS

**G**lumshanks, my imbecile servant, is the perfect example of the stupidity of Trolls. However, their innate love of nasty things makes them useful minions. I barely have to tell them to do anything, since they're always drilling, blowing stuff up, and making a ruckus, anyway.

### Troll Greasemonkeys

Largely useless in battle, this Troll likes to thump things with wrenches.

### Mace Majors

Instead of wrenches, Mace Majors wield large maces. They're still pretty useless.

### Troll Grenadiers

These Trolls have the right idea—find a high spot and lob grenades at any hero-types lurking below.

### Blaster Trolls

These gun-wielding Trolls have the potential to be very useful on the battlefield, if only they didn't take so long to fire.

### Trollverines

Armed with a set of razor-sharp claws, the Trollverines are a valuable addition to my army.

### D. Riveters

These little guys shoot metal from their rivet guns and drop mines on the battlefield.

## Boom Bosses

These goggle-eyed Trolls are equipped with huge handguns that can shoot bouncing bombs.

## Cadet Crushers

Cadet Crushers wield massive enchanted hammers and leave evilized fire in their wake.

## Undead Cadet Crushers

Undead Trolls are just like the living kind. But instead of sickly green flesh, they're all bones.

## Loose Cannons

Loose Cannons are large, explosive, and carry magical shields. Take that, Skylosers!

## Eggsecutioners

These oddball Trolls have chosen to shield themselves with eggshells.

## Troll Welders

Straight from the garage, these Trolls wield blowtorches and welders' masks.

## Missile Maulers

These gun-toting Trolls would be incredibly effective if only they would fire their weapons more often.

# GUIDE TO DROW

The nature-loving goody-goody Elves have always been a thorn in my side, so I was delighted when large numbers of them started converting to the ways of evil and swearing their allegiance to me. Now referred to as Drow, these Darkness-loving former Elves know a thing or two about causing trouble.

## Drow Spearmen

Thanks to their long-handled spears, these Drow warriors don't have to get too close in order to make sure Skylanders get the *point*.

## Goliath Drow

Bigger and stronger than your average Drow, these brutes batter enemies with their spike-covered shields. Unfortunately, they quickly run out of steam.

## Drow Witches

These magically enhanced Drow hurl deadly flying disks at their enemies. They also have very nice hats.

## Blade Witches

When flying disks just aren't damaging enough, the Blade Witches step in with their multi-bladed boomerangs.

## Blitzer Bullies

As big and mean as the Goliath Drow, but equipped with Life Spell Punks on their backs to heal them.

## Drow Archers

These little bowmen are deadly with their bows and arrows.

## Armored Lance Masters

These Drow are decked out in some mean-looking armor, that's for sure.

# GUIDE TO PIRATES

You'll never meet a scurvier band of villains than the pirates who inhabit Skylands. While they aren't technically my minions, we share common goals—doing bad stuff and crushing do-gooders wherever we go.

## Squiddlers

These little squid fellows are armed with guns that shoot exploding blowfish, and I've never met anyone who'd like to be shot with an exploding blowfish.

## Blastaneers

Sticking with the squid theme, the Blastaneers are another pirate type who like to attack from a distance.

**DOOM** FACT

*I do not understand Captain Dreadbeard's love of card games.*

## Squidface Brutes

These big brutes wield giant anchors, and will not hesitate to slam them down on their enemies' unsuspecting heads.

## Seadogs

These large doglike pirates are skilled with their cutlasses and take great pleasure in hacking and chopping at their opponents.

## Captain K9s

These dog creatures served directly under the terrible Captain Dreadbeard. Much like the Squidface Brutes, they enjoy squishing people with giant anchors.

## Pirate Henchmen

Their pink hairdos might look silly, but their curved-bladed clubs only mean business.

# GUIDE TO ARKEYANS

W ay back in the mists of time, the Arkeyans ruled over all of Skylands. Although they weren't all committed to evil—like I am—the worst among them got up to some wonderfully unpleasant stuff. Combining the Elements of Tech and Magic made the Arkeyans immensely powerful, and the more power they gained, the more they wanted.

### Arkeyan Defenders

Armed with a deadly spear, and protected by a shimmering force field, an Arkeyan Defender presents a challenge to even the toughest Skylanders.

**DID YOU KNOW?**
Thanks to the sport of Roboto-Ball, most of the good Arkeyans blew themselves up.

### Arkeyan War Machines

Towering robots built for battle, the War Machines are a testament to the skill of the Arkeyans, and are almost indestructible. Note the word *almost*.

### Arkeyan Ultrons

These robotic warriors may not be the most graceful, but their ability to launch laser-guided missiles more than makes up for their lack of style.

### Arkeyan Jousters

While jousting is a challenging event involving lances and horses, the Arkeyans seemed to believe it involved smashing the ground with heavy weapons. How else do you explain this warrior?

## Arkeyan Shield Juggernauts

Big, strong, and with a shield that can fire deadly energy blasts, it takes a brave soul to face one of these behemoths in battle.

## Arkeyan Cracklers

The ability to create explosive clones of themselves means this villain-type leave their enemies seeing double in more ways than one.

## Arkeyan Rip-Rotors

These little robots may be small, but they're perfect for spinning through the air and smacking the heads of anyone foolish enough to get caught below.

## Arkeyan Knuckledusters

Now these bring back memories. Back when I evilized Glumshanks with a dose of Petrified Darkness, these plasma-blasting minions joined to help him battle the Skylanders. Too bad Glumshanks's incompetence kept them from their moment of glory!

## DOOM FACT

I'll never forgive the Skylanders for taking the Machine of Doom away from me.

## Arkeyan Slamshocks

These villains look like a trash heap from a furnace factory, but when they slam the ground, the effect is pretty shocking!

## Arkeyan Barrelbots

Armed with double-barreled blasters, these robotic minions can pack quite a punch on an unsuspecting Skylander.

# GUIDE TO IMPS AND MABU

The small, mischievous Imps and the dumb, docile Mabu don't have a whole lot in common, other than being common and wimpy. It's a true sign of my incredible generosity that I allow these losers to continue to fight for me. Yes, that's right—bow to KAOS!

### Lockmaster Imps

These tiny critters live inside lock mechanisms, and do their best to prevent anyone from getting them open. Sadly, their best is rarely good enough.

### Flame Imps

One of the smallest of all the Imps, this variety resembles tiny living flames. They attack in large numbers, as on their own they're weak and pointless.

### Rocket Imps

Like most Imps, this yellow-skinned variant is small. Their rocket launchers, though, are anything but. Too bad their rockets are so slow!

### Mabu Warriors

I know you thought the Mabu were all good, but there are a few rotten ones. These carry two swords and travel with company in the alternate reality of the Mirror of Mystery.

### Frozen Fiends

Like Flame Imps, these icy devils are useless on their own. Get enough together, though, and they'll make even the bravest hero's blood run cold.

### Mabu Tanks

Since Mabu aren't the most physically intimidating creatures, even in the Mirror of Mystery, some of them rely on big tanks to do their heavy lifting.

# GUIDE TO K-BOTS AND FEATHERED FIENDS

**W**hat does the *K* in K-Bots stand for? Why, Kaos, of course! These mechanical monsters were built to defend my fortress. I only wish they would do a better job. The same could be said for these foolish birds that begged to come on board for the fight.

### K-Bot Gloopgunners

These robotic guards shoot gloopy green goo on the floor, which slows enemies down . . . and which I make Glumshanks clean up afterward.

### Raven Lobbers

These nasty green birds carry mortars on their shoulders and fire three shots at a time. They're quick and sharp!

### DID YOU KNOW?
The cry of the Birdbarian is one of the most annoying sounds in Skylands.

### K-Bot Mineminers

Equipped with homing missiles, electroshock powers, and ground-slam attacks, these K-Bots are the most dangerous guards in the fortress.

### Birdbarians

Birdbarians are shrieking, spinning, scimitar-wielding terrors. Sometimes all that spinning makes them a little dizzy.

### K-Bot Splodeshards

These little bots usually hang around the fortress minding their own business. When they detect an intruder, though, their drills spin into action and they charge at the closest pair of legs.

# GUIDE TO TROGS AND GREEBLES

Trogs are some of the rarest baddies in all of Skylands. Greebles, on the other hand, are much more common—so much so that evildoers can order them to be delivered by the dozen, to help them out with their latest wicked schemes.

### Trog Pinchers

Small, chunky, and hunched over, these unpleasant brutes don't pinch, like their name suggests, but instead swipe at their enemies with crystal blades.

### Trog Wanderers

This Trog-type isn't much of a threat until it gets hit. As soon as it does, it shrinks, races at the closest hero, and bites them hard on the bottom.

**DID YOU KNOW?**

Glumshanks gets the heebie-jeebies when he looks into a Trog's empty, soulless eyes.

### Trogmanders

The wizards of the Trog race, the Trogmanders can make Trog Pinchers grow to a great height, making them much more dangerous.

### Greeble Screwballs

These little goblin-like fiends are each equipped with a homemade launcher that fires huge rocks into the air, which then fall down on anyone below.

## Greeble Blunderbusses

These fiends are each armed with blunderbuss guns with which they can target any nearby heroic sorts. I once evilized a whole pack of them at once!

## Greeble Ironclads

Large, armored, and violent, these Greebles prefer fists over firearms. Their punches hit like wrecking balls, but they have a habit of falling over at the worst possible moments.

## Greeble Heavers

Heavers are able to attack from a distance, thanks to their incredibly accurate projectile-firing weapon.

### DOOM FACT

I once received a free hat with my Greeble order! Too bad it was a LAME hat.

## Bubba Greebs

An enormous mutant Greeble that my mother decided to keep as a pet. Of course, he wouldn't have fallen to those stupid Skylanders if *I* had been in charge of him.

## Pirate Powderkegs

A Greeble that is also a pirate? Believe it! First, it attacks with a cannon, then it steals all the treasure. Charming!

## Pirate Slamspins

These Greebles like to spin themselves dizzy while holding sharp spears. Strange methods, but as long as they get the job done . . .

# GUIDE TO CHOMPIES

Chompies are everywhere in Skylands. They're small and stupid, but their sheer numbers makes them a great asset to me when I need cheap soldiers.

### Crunchers

These little beasts sink their teeth into their victim and refuse to let go.

### Frigid Chompies

This variety doesn't just munch on their victims—they freeze them first to lock in the freshness.

### Armored Chompies

The clue's in the name—Chompies wearing armor. It makes them look adorable, actually.

### Chompy Bot 9000

Not a Chompy so much as a giant Chompy-shaped machine, piloted by a Chompy, which fires Chompies from its arms.

### Chompy Powerhouses

These Chompies have managed to get their hands on (and in) some heavy metal gauntlets.

### Chompy Rustbuds

Robotic Chompies made largely from pieces of scrap metal.

### Chompy Blitzblooms

Faster and more colorful than your average Chompy.

### Chompy Boomblossoms

Part Chompy, part high-powered explosive.

### Goo Chompies

Exposure to some deeply unpleasant toxic waste has granted these Chompies the power to turn into ... um ... lumps of goo.

### Mega Chompies

You don't want to see what happens when Chompies get together. It involves belly flops and shockwaves.

### En Fuego Chompies

Fiery Chompies that explode. Simple, yet beautiful.

**DOOM** FACT

My fool mother never let me have a pet Chompy growing up.

### Pirate Chompies

*Arrr!* What makes these seafarin' Chompies different from their typical brethren? Style, of course!

### Chompy Frostflowers

Using ice as armor is a pretty nifty innovation for something as simpleminded as a Chompy.

### Chompy Pastepetals

It is so fun to see the Skylanders' faces when the Pastepetals split into two and attack from both sides!

### Chompy Pods

Normally I find nature to be unbearably stupid, but I do admire Chompy Pods. They're like little Chompy factories.

# GUIDE TO EVILIKIN

When I was merely a young future ultimate evil overlord of ultimate evil, I created a group of weak and stupid servants out of wood and called them Wilikin. Once they were evilized, they turned into delightfully demonic minions!

### Evilikin Cannons

What's more frightening than a magically animated wooden monster? A magically animated wooden monster *who can shoot cannonballs from its mouth!*

**DOOM** FACT

*I may call them "kin," but these idiots are no family of mine.*

### Evilikin Spinners

Equipped with razor-sharp blades on the ends of their arms, these Evilikin spin around at breakneck speeds, slashing anyone who dares to get too close.

### Woodensteins

Woodensteins are painfully slow, yes—but one blow from these massive monstrosities and it's all over for their enemies.

# GUIDE TO UNDEAD FORCES

ew would disagree that the Undead Element is the creepiest Element of all, and the same can be said for the villain-types aligned with it. I would caution you to read no further . . . however, I do quite enjoy giving people nightmares!

### Rotting Robbies

Chomping, swiping, decomposing zombies, the Rotting Robbies attack with clawed hands and rotten teeth. They also smell terrible.

### Bone 'n' Arrows

You'd think having no eyes would pose a problem when it came to shooting arrows, but these skeletal archers have no problem hitting their targets.

### Rhu-Babies

These little beasts may only be Chompy-size, but they make Chompies seem absolutely adorable in comparison.

### DID YOU KNOW?

I once built a machine that could extract the Undead from Undead Skylanders!

### Rhu-Barbs

Rhu-Babies are tiny, and pose little danger on their own. With the help of a Spell Punk, though, they can turn into hulking Rhu-Barbs and dish out much more damage.

### Shield Skeletons

Skeletons with shields. I can't really spell it out any more clearly than that. It's right there in the name.

# GUIDE TO MINIONS

I n one of my most clever schemes, I created evil duplicates of some of the Skylanders, like the ones below.

### Evil Missile Minion

A duplicate of the Skylander Zook, this minion is better in every way, with the ability to create mushroom shields, and far superior weaponry.

### Evil Knight Minion

This clone of the Skylander Chop Chop dishes out punishment with his flaming sword, and deflects attacks with his spiked shield.

### Evil Ice Yeti

Picture the furry blue Skylander Slam Bam. Now picture him evil. Congratulations, you just pictured the Evil Ice Yeti, who takes down enemies with heavy punches and even heavier shards of ice.

### Evil Pyro Archer

Always on the move, this Flameslinger duplicate fires off five arrows in a row, before dashing to another spot and opening fire once more.

### Evil Phoenix Dragon

With the ability to teleport, breathe flame, and set fire to Skylanders' feet, this evil clone of Sunburn is one of the most effective of all the doubles.

### Evil Witch Minion

The Skylander Hex always looked quite evil to me, so I was surprised to find out she wasn't. Her double definitely is, though, and its Undead magical bolts prove a real challenge for the heroes.

### Evil Amphibious Gillman

Based on the Skylander Gill Grunt, this duplicate can fire three harpoons at the same time, while zooming around on a Water-powered jet pack.

### Evil Water Dragon

While the Skylander Zap may be a noble and trustworthy sort, his double is just the opposite. With its ability to spit thunderbolts, it has come very close to stopping the heroes in their tracks.

### DOOM FACT

I would make a duplicate of Roller Brawl, but I'm afraid she would get hurt.

### Evil Imp Minion

This minion has only mastered one of Ghost Roaster's attacks. Despite that, its giant chomping skull really puts the *bite* on the Skylanders. See what I did there?

### Evil Eruptor

A near-identical clone of Eruptor, complete with Magma Ball attack and the ability to vomit lava, this clone is the most powerful of them all!

# GUIDE TO GEARGOLEMS

M any evil geniuses would happily throw scrap metal away, but I have always been smart and resourceful. These Geargolems emerged from worthless trash to become an army of mechanical minions.

### Fire Geargolems

The Fire Geargolem has a devastating flamethrower attack, and also looks very impressive at night.

### Air Geargolems

Hovering around on a mini tornado, these Geargolems use their Air-powered abilities to suck in any nearby Skylanders.

### Ice Geargolems

These ice-coated minions can fire three icicles at a time at their enemies.

### Tech Geargolems

Get too close to one of these and they'll fire a barrage of nuts and bolts that will leave you battered and bruised.

### Earth Geargolems

The Earth Geargolem attacks by slamming its mechanical fists, sending out rippling shockwaves.

### Vortex Geargolems

These brutes are like Air Geargolems that can summon Cyclopses.

### Clock Geargolems

These time-aligned minions spin and can only be harmed when time itself is stopped.

# GUIDE TO GRUMBLEBUMS, STITCHED ENEMIES, AND THE REANIMATED

As you've seen, Skylands is filled with all sorts of delightful evil creatures, some more common than others. I'll wrap up my guide with some miscellaneous oddball villains that I have had the distinct displeasure of commanding in combat!

## Grumblebum Thrashers

As they spend most of their time in Mudwater Hollow, it's difficult to tell exactly how hideous Grumblebums are. They might be completely grotesque, or they may just be covered in murky Mudwater-goo.

### DOOM FACT

*An evil genius can't be too picky about the minions he sacrifices for the cause.*

## Snozzlers

Much like the friendly elephants that inhabit your world, Snozzlers have long trunks and floppy ears. Unlike elephants, they fly and attack Skylanders with spitballs.

## Cuddles

Aww, what a friendly name! But when this beastly creature reaches out, you'd be wise to step back. Its arms—and sharp fingers—can reach surprisingly far.

## Ooglers

These little pests look like they're made out of light. They can shoot orbs from their eyes that stay connected by a damaging force field as they sweep around the battlefield.

## Transformed Barrels

Though these creatures once were barrels, they are now vicious, bomb-throwing menaces that sneak up out of nowhere.

# FAREWELL!

**S**o, POSER Master, the time has come to bid you farewell. And not a moment too soon, as far as I'm concerned.

I am certain you will have learned much from the great wisdom of Kaos. I am not so certain, however, that your puny little brain will be able to hold on to much of what you have learned, so I order you to immediately go back to the beginning and read this book again. Twice!

Now, if you don't mind (or even if you do), I must go and make plans to conquer Skylands and rid the place of those irritating excuses for heroes once and for all. Before I go, though, perhaps Glumshanks would like to say a few words?

Why thank you, Lord Kaos, that's very—

**S**ILENCE, FOOL! That's quite enough, Glumshanks. Now get back to work! And you, reader, get back to the start of this book. It isn't going to read itself, you know. And remember, I'll be conquering you all soon! TA-TA!